50 Summer Season Recipes for Home

By: Kelly Johnson

Table of Contents

- Caprese Salad
- Grilled Chicken Skewers
- Corn on the Cob with Herb Butter
- Watermelon Feta Salad
- Lemon Herb Grilled Salmon
- Tomato Basil Bruschetta
- Peach and Prosciutto Salad
- Avocado Gazpacho
- Pineapple Salsa
- BBQ Pulled Pork Sandwiches
- Zucchini Noodles with Pesto
- Greek Chicken Gyros
- Strawberry Spinach Salad
- Chicken and Vegetable Kabobs
- Grilled Portobello Mushrooms
- Spicy Shrimp Tacos
- Cucumber Mint Lemonade
- Summer Berry Smoothie
- Lemon Basil Pasta Salad
- Mango Avocado Salsa
- Roasted Beet and Goat Cheese Salad
- Grilled Vegetable Platter
- Caprese Stuffed Avocados
- Chilled Cucumber Soup
- Fruit Salad with Honey Lime Dressing
- Smoked Salmon and Cream Cheese Wraps
- Grilled Peach Salad
- Roasted Garlic Hummus
- Classic Coleslaw
- Basil Pesto Pasta
- Buffalo Chicken Lettuce Wraps
- Marinated Tomato Salad
- Coconut Lime Chicken
- Sliced Tomato and Burrata Salad
- Grilled Shrimp and Pineapple Skewers
- Corn and Black Bean Salad

- Chilled Gazpacho
- Herbed Lemon Chicken
- Tomato Mozzarella Skewers
- Peach Iced Tea
- Tropical Smoothie Bowl
- Grilled Teriyaki Chicken
- Sweet Corn Salad
- Chicken Caesar Wraps
- Strawberry Shortcake
- Avocado and Tomato Quesadillas
- Grilled Lobster Tails
- Mango Coconut Chia Pudding
- Ginger Peach Salsa
- Lemon Blueberry Muffins

Caprese Salad

Ingredients:

- **4 ripe tomatoes**, sliced
- **8 ounces fresh mozzarella cheese**, sliced
- **1/4 cup fresh basil leaves**
- **2 tablespoons extra virgin olive oil**
- **1 tablespoon balsamic vinegar** (optional)
- **Salt and pepper to taste**

Instructions:

1. **Assemble the Salad:**
   - On a serving platter, arrange the tomato and mozzarella slices alternately, slightly overlapping them.
   - Tuck fresh basil leaves between the slices of tomato and mozzarella.
2. **Dress the Salad:**
   - Drizzle the extra virgin olive oil over the salad.
   - If using balsamic vinegar, drizzle it over as well.
3. **Season:**
   - Sprinkle with salt and freshly ground black pepper to taste.
4. **Serve:**
   - Serve immediately as a fresh appetizer or side dish.

Enjoy your Caprese Salad!

Grilled Chicken Skewers

Ingredients:

For the Marinade:

- **1/4 cup olive oil**
- **1/4 cup soy sauce**
- **2 tablespoons lemon juice**
- **2 tablespoons honey**
- **3 cloves garlic**, minced
- **1 tablespoon grated fresh ginger** (optional)
- **1 teaspoon dried oregano**
- **1 teaspoon paprika**
- **Salt and pepper to taste**

For the Skewers:

- **1 lb (450g) boneless, skinless chicken breasts**, cut into bite-sized pieces
- **1 red bell pepper**, cut into chunks
- **1 yellow bell pepper**, cut into chunks
- **1 medium onion**, cut into chunks
- **1 zucchini**, sliced into rounds
- **Wooden or metal skewers** (if using wooden skewers, soak them in water for at least 30 minutes before grilling)

Instructions:

1. **Prepare the Marinade:**
    - In a bowl, whisk together the olive oil, soy sauce, lemon juice, honey, garlic, grated ginger (if using), oregano, paprika, salt, and pepper.
2. **Marinate the Chicken:**
    - Place the chicken pieces in a large resealable plastic bag or shallow dish. Pour the marinade over the chicken, making sure all pieces are coated.
    - Seal the bag or cover the dish and refrigerate for at least 30 minutes to 2 hours for best flavor.
3. **Prepare the Skewers:**
    - Thread the marinated chicken pieces onto the skewers, alternating with chunks of bell peppers, onion, and zucchini.
4. **Grill the Skewers:**
    - Preheat your grill to medium-high heat.
    - Place the skewers on the grill and cook for about 10-15 minutes, turning occasionally, until the chicken is cooked through and has an internal temperature of 165°F (74°C) and the vegetables are tender and slightly charred.
5. **Serve:**

- Remove the skewers from the grill and let them rest for a few minutes.
- Serve the grilled chicken skewers with your favorite side dishes or over a bed of rice or quinoa.

Enjoy your flavorful and juicy Grilled Chicken Skewers!

Corn on the Cob with Herb Butter

Ingredients:

For the Corn:

- **4 ears of fresh corn on the cob**, husked and cleaned
- **Salt**, for boiling

For the Herb Butter:

- **1/2 cup (1 stick) unsalted butter**, softened
- **2 tablespoons fresh parsley**, finely chopped
- **1 tablespoon fresh chives**, finely chopped
- **1 tablespoon fresh basil**, finely chopped (optional)
- **1 clove garlic**, minced
- **1 teaspoon lemon zest**
- **Salt and pepper to taste**

Instructions:

1. **Prepare the Herb Butter:**
    - In a bowl, combine the softened butter, parsley, chives, basil (if using), minced garlic, and lemon zest.
    - Season with salt and pepper to taste. Mix well until all ingredients are thoroughly combined.
    - Transfer the herb butter to a piece of plastic wrap or parchment paper. Roll it into a log and refrigerate until firm.
2. **Cook the Corn:**
    - Bring a large pot of water to a boil. Add a pinch of salt.
    - Add the husked corn to the boiling water. Cook for 7-10 minutes, or until the corn is tender.
    - Remove the corn from the water and let it drain.
3. **Serve:**
    - Once the corn is cool enough to handle, spread the chilled herb butter over the hot corn.
    - Serve immediately, garnished with extra herbs if desired.

Enjoy your delicious Corn on the Cob with Herb Butter!

Watermelon Feta Salad

Ingredients:

- **4 cups seedless watermelon**, cut into bite-sized cubes
- **1 cup feta cheese**, crumbled
- **1/4 cup fresh mint leaves**, chopped
- **1/4 cup red onion**, thinly sliced (optional)
- **2 tablespoons extra virgin olive oil**
- **1 tablespoon balsamic vinegar** or **lime juice**
- **Salt and pepper to taste**

Instructions:

1. **Combine Ingredients:**
   - In a large bowl, gently toss the watermelon cubes, crumbled feta cheese, chopped mint leaves, and red onion (if using).
2. **Dress the Salad:**
   - Drizzle the olive oil and balsamic vinegar (or lime juice) over the salad.
   - Season with salt and pepper to taste.
3. **Toss and Serve:**
   - Gently toss the salad to combine all ingredients.
   - Serve immediately or chill for 30 minutes to enhance the flavors.

Enjoy your refreshing Watermelon Feta Salad!

Lemon Herb Grilled Salmon

Ingredients:

- **4 salmon fillets** (about 6 oz each), skin on or off
- **2 tablespoons olive oil**
- **2 tablespoons lemon juice** (about 1 lemon)
- **3 cloves garlic**, minced
- **1 tablespoon fresh parsley**, chopped (or 1 teaspoon dried parsley)
- **1 tablespoon fresh dill**, chopped (or 1 teaspoon dried dill)
- **1 teaspoon dried oregano**
- **Salt and pepper to taste**
- **Lemon wedges** (for serving)

Instructions:

1. **Prepare the Marinade:**
   - In a small bowl, whisk together the olive oil, lemon juice, minced garlic, parsley, dill, oregano, salt, and pepper.
2. **Marinate the Salmon:**
   - Place the salmon fillets in a shallow dish or a resealable plastic bag.
   - Pour the marinade over the salmon, making sure each fillet is evenly coated.
   - Cover or seal and refrigerate for 15-30 minutes.
3. **Preheat the Grill:**
   - Preheat your grill to medium-high heat.
4. **Grill the Salmon:**
   - Oil the grill grates or use a grill basket to prevent sticking.
   - Place the marinated salmon fillets on the grill, skin-side down if applicable.
   - Grill for about 4-6 minutes per side, or until the salmon is opaque and flakes easily with a fork. Cooking time may vary depending on the thickness of the fillets.
5. **Serve:**
   - Remove the salmon from the grill and let it rest for a few minutes.
   - Serve with lemon wedges on the side.

Enjoy your flavorful Lemon Herb Grilled Salmon!

Tomato Basil Bruschetta

Ingredients:

- **1 baguette**, sliced into 1/2-inch rounds
- **4 ripe tomatoes**, diced
- **1/4 cup fresh basil**, chopped
- **2 cloves garlic**, minced
- **2 tablespoons extra virgin olive oil**
- **1 tablespoon balsamic vinegar** (optional)
- **Salt and pepper to taste**

Instructions:

1. **Prepare the Toast:**
    - Preheat your oven to 400°F (200°C).
    - Arrange the baguette slices on a baking sheet. Brush lightly with olive oil.
    - Toast in the oven for 5-7 minutes, or until golden and crispy.
2. **Prepare the Topping:**
    - In a bowl, combine the diced tomatoes, chopped basil, minced garlic, olive oil, and balsamic vinegar (if using).
    - Season with salt and pepper to taste.
3. **Assemble:**
    - Spoon the tomato mixture onto the toasted baguette slices.
4. **Serve:**
    - Serve immediately as an appetizer or snack.

Enjoy your delicious Tomato Basil Bruschetta!

Peach and Prosciutto Salad

Ingredients:

- **4 ripe peaches**, sliced
- **4 ounces prosciutto**, thinly sliced
- **4 cups mixed salad greens** (such as arugula or spinach)
- **1/4 cup crumbled feta cheese** or **goat cheese**
- **1/4 cup toasted almonds** or **walnuts**
- **2 tablespoons extra virgin olive oil**
- **1 tablespoon balsamic vinegar**
- **1 teaspoon honey** (optional)
- **Salt and pepper to taste**

Instructions:

1. **Prepare the Salad:**
   - On a serving platter or individual plates, arrange the mixed salad greens.
   - Top with sliced peaches, prosciutto, crumbled cheese, and toasted nuts.
2. **Make the Dressing:**
   - In a small bowl, whisk together olive oil, balsamic vinegar, and honey (if using). Season with salt and pepper to taste.
3. **Dress the Salad:**
   - Drizzle the dressing over the salad just before serving.
4. **Serve:**
   - Serve immediately for the freshest flavor.

Enjoy your Peach and Prosciutto Salad!

Avocado Gazpacho

Ingredients:

- **2 ripe avocados**, peeled and pitted
- **1 cucumber**, peeled and chopped
- **1 green bell pepper**, chopped
- **1 small onion**, chopped
- **2 cloves garlic**, minced
- **2 cups vegetable or chicken broth**
- **1/4 cup fresh lime juice** (about 2 limes)
- **2 tablespoons olive oil**
- **Salt and pepper to taste**
- **Fresh cilantro** or **parsley** (for garnish, optional)

Instructions:

1. **Blend Ingredients:**
    - In a blender or food processor, combine the avocados, cucumber, green bell pepper, onion, garlic, and half of the broth.
    - Blend until smooth.
2. **Adjust Consistency:**
    - Gradually add the remaining broth until you reach your desired consistency.
3. **Season:**
    - Stir in the lime juice and olive oil.
    - Season with salt and pepper to taste.
4. **Chill and Serve:**
    - Refrigerate for at least 1 hour to chill and let the flavors meld.
    - Garnish with fresh cilantro or parsley if desired before serving.

Enjoy your creamy and cool Avocado Gazpacho!

Pineapple Salsa

Ingredients:

- **2 cups fresh pineapple**, finely diced
- **1/2 red onion**, finely chopped
- **1/2 red bell pepper**, finely chopped
- **1 jalapeño**, seeded and minced (optional, for heat)
- **1/4 cup fresh cilantro**, chopped
- **1 tablespoon lime juice** (about 1 lime)
- **Salt to taste**

Instructions:

1. **Combine Ingredients:**
   - In a bowl, mix together the diced pineapple, red onion, red bell pepper, jalapeño (if using), and cilantro.
2. **Add Lime Juice:**
   - Stir in the lime juice and season with salt to taste.
3. **Chill:**
   - Let the salsa sit for at least 15 minutes to allow the flavors to meld.
4. **Serve:**
   - Serve as a fresh topping for grilled meats, fish, or with tortilla chips.

Enjoy your refreshing Pineapple Salsa!

BBQ Pulled Pork Sandwiches

Ingredients:

For the Pulled Pork:

- **4-5 lbs (1.8-2.3 kg) pork shoulder** (also known as pork butt)
- **1 tablespoon paprika**
- **1 tablespoon brown sugar**
- **1 teaspoon garlic powder**
- **1 teaspoon onion powder**
- **1 teaspoon ground cumin**
- **1/2 teaspoon cayenne pepper** (optional, for heat)
- **Salt and black pepper to taste**
- **1 cup BBQ sauce** (store-bought or homemade)
- **1 cup chicken or vegetable broth**

For Serving:

- **Hamburger buns** or **sandwich rolls**
- **Coleslaw** (optional, for topping)

Instructions:

1. **Prepare the Pork:**
   - In a small bowl, mix paprika, brown sugar, garlic powder, onion powder, ground cumin, cayenne pepper, salt, and black pepper.
   - Rub this spice mixture all over the pork shoulder.
2. **Cook the Pork:**
   - **Slow Cooker Method:** Place the seasoned pork shoulder in the slow cooker. Pour the chicken or vegetable broth around the pork. Cover and cook on low for 8-10 hours, or until the pork is tender and easily shreds with a fork.
   - **Oven Method:** Preheat your oven to 300°F (150°C). Place the seasoned pork shoulder in a roasting pan. Pour the chicken or vegetable broth into the pan. Cover tightly with foil and roast for 4-5 hours, or until the pork is tender and easily shreds with a fork.
3. **Shred the Pork:**
   - Once the pork is cooked, remove it from the slow cooker or oven and transfer it to a large bowl. Use two forks to shred the pork into bite-sized pieces.
   - Stir in the BBQ sauce until the pork is well coated.
4. **Assemble the Sandwiches:**
   - Toast the hamburger buns or sandwich rolls if desired.
   - Pile the pulled pork onto the bottom half of each bun. Top with coleslaw if desired.
   - Place the top half of the bun on top and serve.

Enjoy your delicious BBQ Pulled Pork Sandwiches!

Zucchini Noodles with Pesto

Ingredients:

For the Zucchini Noodles:

- **4 medium zucchinis**, spiralized into noodles
- **1 tablespoon olive oil**
- **Salt and pepper to taste**

For the Pesto:

- **1 cup fresh basil leaves**
- **1/4 cup pine nuts** (or walnuts)
- **1/4 cup grated Parmesan cheese**
- **2 cloves garlic**
- **1/4 cup extra virgin olive oil**
- **Salt and pepper to taste**

Instructions:

1. **Prepare the Pesto:**
    - In a food processor or blender, combine basil leaves, pine nuts, Parmesan cheese, and garlic.
    - Pulse until the ingredients are finely chopped.
    - With the processor running, slowly drizzle in the olive oil until the pesto is smooth and well combined.
    - Season with salt and pepper to taste. Set aside.
2. **Cook the Zucchini Noodles:**
    - Heat olive oil in a large skillet over medium heat.
    - Add the zucchini noodles and sauté for about 2-4 minutes, just until tender but still slightly crisp. Avoid overcooking to keep the noodles from becoming mushy.
    - Season with salt and pepper.
3. **Combine and Serve:**
    - Toss the cooked zucchini noodles with the prepared pesto until well coated.
    - Serve immediately, garnished with additional Parmesan cheese or fresh basil if desired.

Enjoy your Zucchini Noodles with Pesto!

Greek Chicken Gyros

Ingredients:

For the Chicken Marinade:

- **1 lb (450g) boneless, skinless chicken thighs**, cut into strips
- **1/4 cup olive oil**
- **3 tablespoons lemon juice** (about 1 lemon)
- **3 cloves garlic**, minced
- **2 teaspoons dried oregano**
- **1 teaspoon ground cumin**
- **1 teaspoon paprika**
- **Salt and pepper to taste**

For the Tzatziki Sauce:

- **1 cup Greek yogurt**
- **1/2 cucumber**, peeled, seeded, and finely grated
- **2 cloves garlic**, minced
- **1 tablespoon fresh dill**, chopped (or 1 teaspoon dried dill)
- **1 tablespoon lemon juice**
- **Salt and pepper to taste**

For Serving:

- **Pita bread** or **flatbreads**
- **Sliced tomatoes**
- **Sliced red onions**
- **Shredded lettuce**
- **Sliced cucumbers**

Instructions:

1. **Marinate the Chicken:**
   - In a bowl, combine the olive oil, lemon juice, minced garlic, dried oregano, ground cumin, paprika, salt, and pepper.
   - Add the chicken strips and toss to coat. Cover and refrigerate for at least 30 minutes, or up to 4 hours for best results.
2. **Prepare the Tzatziki Sauce:**
   - In a mixing bowl, combine Greek yogurt, grated cucumber (squeeze out excess moisture), minced garlic, fresh dill, and lemon juice.
   - Season with salt and pepper to taste. Mix well and refrigerate until ready to use.
3. **Cook the Chicken:**
   - Preheat your grill or a grill pan over medium-high heat.

- Grill the chicken strips for about 5-7 minutes per side, or until fully cooked and slightly charred. The internal temperature should reach 165°F (74°C).
4. **Assemble the Gyros:**
    - Warm the pita bread or flatbreads on the grill or in a dry skillet.
    - Spread a generous amount of tzatziki sauce on each pita.
    - Top with grilled chicken, sliced tomatoes, red onions, shredded lettuce, and sliced cucumbers.
5. **Serve:**
    - Fold the pita or flatbread around the fillings and serve immediately.

Enjoy your homemade Greek Chicken Gyros!

Strawberry Spinach Salad

Ingredients:

- **4 cups fresh spinach leaves**
- **1 cup fresh strawberries**, sliced
- **1/4 cup red onion**, thinly sliced
- **1/4 cup crumbled feta cheese** (or goat cheese)
- **1/4 cup sliced almonds** (toasted if desired)

For the Dressing:

- **2 tablespoons balsamic vinegar**
- **1 tablespoon honey**
- **1/4 cup extra virgin olive oil**
- **Salt and pepper to taste**

Instructions:

1. **Prepare the Dressing:**
   - In a small bowl or jar, whisk together balsamic vinegar, honey, and olive oil.
   - Season with salt and pepper to taste. Set aside.
2. **Assemble the Salad:**
   - In a large salad bowl, combine spinach leaves, sliced strawberries, red onion, crumbled feta cheese, and sliced almonds.
3. **Dress the Salad:**
   - Drizzle the dressing over the salad just before serving.
   - Toss gently to coat all ingredients evenly.
4. **Serve:**
   - Serve immediately to enjoy the fresh flavors.

Enjoy your Strawberry Spinach Salad!

Chicken and Vegetable Kabobs

Ingredients:

- **1 lb (450g) boneless, skinless chicken breasts**, cut into bite-sized pieces
- **1 red bell pepper**, cut into chunks
- **1 yellow bell pepper**, cut into chunks
- **1 zucchini**, sliced into rounds
- **1 red onion**, cut into chunks
- **1 cup cherry tomatoes**
- **2 tablespoons olive oil**
- **2 tablespoons lemon juice**
- **3 cloves garlic**, minced
- **1 tablespoon dried oregano** or **1 tablespoon fresh oregano**, chopped
- **1 teaspoon paprika**
- **Salt and pepper to taste**
- **Wooden or metal skewers** (if using wooden skewers, soak them in water for at least 30 minutes before grilling)

Instructions:

1. **Prepare the Marinade:**
   - In a bowl, mix together olive oil, lemon juice, minced garlic, dried oregano, paprika, salt, and pepper.
2. **Marinate the Chicken:**
   - Place the chicken pieces in a large resealable plastic bag or shallow dish.
   - Pour the marinade over the chicken, making sure all pieces are well coated.
   - Seal the bag or cover the dish and refrigerate for at least 30 minutes, or up to 2 hours for best flavor.
3. **Assemble the Kabobs:**
   - Thread the marinated chicken pieces onto skewers, alternating with chunks of bell peppers, zucchini, red onion, and cherry tomatoes.
4. **Grill the Kabobs:**
   - Preheat your grill to medium-high heat.
   - Lightly oil the grill grates or use a grill basket to prevent sticking.
   - Place the skewers on the grill and cook for about 10-15 minutes, turning occasionally, until the chicken is cooked through and has an internal temperature of 165°F (74°C) and the vegetables are tender.
5. **Serve:**
   - Remove the kabobs from the grill and let them rest for a few minutes.
   - Serve with your favorite side dishes or over a bed of rice or quinoa.

Enjoy your flavorful Chicken and Vegetable Kabobs!

Grilled Portobello Mushrooms

Ingredients:

- **4 large Portobello mushrooms**, stems removed
- **1/4 cup extra virgin olive oil**
- **2 tablespoons balsamic vinegar**
- **2 cloves garlic**, minced
- **1 tablespoon fresh rosemary**, chopped (or 1 teaspoon dried rosemary)
- **1 teaspoon dried thyme**
- **Salt and pepper to taste**

Instructions:

1. **Prepare the Marinade:**
    - In a small bowl, whisk together olive oil, balsamic vinegar, minced garlic, rosemary, thyme, salt, and pepper.
2. **Marinate the Mushrooms:**
    - Brush the Portobello mushrooms with the marinade on both sides.
    - Let them marinate for about 15-30 minutes to absorb the flavors.
3. **Preheat the Grill:**
    - Preheat your grill to medium-high heat.
4. **Grill the Mushrooms:**
    - Place the marinated mushrooms on the grill, gill side up.
    - Grill for about 4-5 minutes per side, or until the mushrooms are tender and have nice grill marks.
5. **Serve:**
    - Remove from the grill and let them rest for a few minutes.
    - Serve as a side dish, on a bun as a burger substitute, or sliced over salads and pasta.

Enjoy your savory and satisfying Grilled Portobello Mushrooms!

Spicy Shrimp Tacos

Ingredients:

For the Spicy Shrimp:

- **1 lb (450g) large shrimp**, peeled and deveined
- **2 tablespoons olive oil**
- **2 tablespoons chili powder**
- **1 teaspoon paprika**
- **1 teaspoon ground cumin**
- **1/2 teaspoon garlic powder**
- **1/2 teaspoon onion powder**
- **1/4 teaspoon cayenne pepper** (adjust to taste)
- **Salt and pepper to taste**
- **1 tablespoon lime juice** (about 1 lime)

For the Slaw:

- **2 cups shredded cabbage** (green or red)
- **1 cup shredded carrots**
- **1/4 cup chopped fresh cilantro**
- **1 tablespoon lime juice**
- **1 tablespoon honey**
- **Salt and pepper to taste**

For Serving:

- **8 small corn or flour tortillas**
- **Fresh cilantro**, chopped (for garnish)
- **Lime wedges** (for serving)
- **Sour cream** or **Greek yogurt** (optional, for topping)

Instructions:

1. **Prepare the Spicy Shrimp:**
   - In a bowl, combine olive oil, chili powder, paprika, cumin, garlic powder, onion powder, cayenne pepper, salt, pepper, and lime juice.
   - Add the shrimp and toss to coat evenly.
   - Let marinate for 15-30 minutes if time allows.
2. **Cook the Shrimp:**
   - Preheat a grill or skillet over medium-high heat.
   - Cook the shrimp for about 2-3 minutes per side, or until they are pink and opaque.
3. **Prepare the Slaw:**

        - In a large bowl, combine shredded cabbage, shredded carrots, and chopped cilantro.
        - In a small bowl, whisk together lime juice and honey.
        - Pour the dressing over the slaw and toss to combine. Season with salt and pepper to taste.
4. **Warm the Tortillas:**
        - Heat the tortillas on a dry skillet or grill until warm and pliable.
5. **Assemble the Tacos:**
        - Place a few shrimp on each tortilla.
        - Top with slaw and garnish with fresh cilantro.
        - Serve with lime wedges and sour cream or Greek yogurt if desired.

Enjoy your spicy and delicious Shrimp Tacos!

Cucumber Mint Lemonade

Ingredients:

- **1 large cucumber**, peeled and sliced
- **1 cup fresh mint leaves**
- **1 cup fresh lemon juice** (about 4-6 lemons)
- **1/2 cup honey** or **sugar** (adjust to taste)
- **4 cups cold water**
- **Ice cubes**
- **Lemon slices** and **mint sprigs** for garnish (optional)

Instructions:

1. **Make Cucumber Mint Infusion:**
   - In a blender, combine the cucumber slices and mint leaves. Blend until smooth.
   - Strain the mixture through a fine mesh sieve or cheesecloth into a large pitcher, pressing down to extract as much liquid as possible.
2. **Prepare Lemonade:**
   - In the pitcher with the cucumber mint infusion, add fresh lemon juice and honey (or sugar). Stir until the honey or sugar is completely dissolved.
3. **Add Water:**
   - Pour in the cold water and stir well to combine.
4. **Serve:**
   - Chill the lemonade in the refrigerator for at least 1 hour.
   - Serve over ice, garnished with lemon slices and mint sprigs if desired.

Enjoy your cool and refreshing Cucumber Mint Lemonade!

Summer Berry Smoothie

Ingredients:

- **1 cup fresh or frozen mixed berries** (such as strawberries, blueberries, raspberries, and blackberries)
- **1 banana**, peeled
- **1/2 cup Greek yogurt** or **regular yogurt** (plain or vanilla)
- **1/2 cup orange juice** (or any other fruit juice)
- **1/2 cup milk** or **almond milk** (adjust for desired thickness)
- **1 tablespoon honey** or **maple syrup** (optional, for extra sweetness)
- **1/2 cup ice cubes** (if using fresh berries)

Instructions:

1. **Blend Ingredients:**
   - In a blender, combine the mixed berries, banana, Greek yogurt, orange juice, milk, and honey (if using).
   - Blend until smooth. If the smoothie is too thick, add more milk or juice to reach your desired consistency.
2. **Add Ice (Optional):**
   - If you're using fresh berries and want a colder, thicker smoothie, add ice cubes and blend again until smooth.
3. **Serve:**
   - Pour the smoothie into glasses and serve immediately.
4. **Garnish (Optional):**
   - Garnish with additional berries or a mint sprig for a nice touch.

Enjoy your delicious and refreshing Summer Berry Smoothie!

Lemon Basil Pasta Salad

Ingredients:

- **8 oz (225g) pasta** (such as rotini, penne, or farfalle)
- **1 cup cherry tomatoes**, halved
- **1/2 cup cucumber**, diced
- **1/4 cup red onion**, finely chopped
- **1/4 cup fresh basil leaves**, chopped
- **1/4 cup grated Parmesan cheese**

For the Lemon Dressing:

- **1/4 cup extra virgin olive oil**
- **2 tablespoons fresh lemon juice** (about 1 lemon)
- **1 teaspoon lemon zest**
- **1 clove garlic**, minced
- **1 teaspoon Dijon mustard**
- **Salt and pepper to taste**

Instructions:

1. **Cook the Pasta:**
   - Cook the pasta according to the package instructions until al dente. Drain and rinse under cold water to cool.
2. **Prepare the Dressing:**
   - In a small bowl or jar, whisk together olive oil, lemon juice, lemon zest, minced garlic, Dijon mustard, salt, and pepper until well combined.
3. **Combine Salad Ingredients:**
   - In a large bowl, toss the cooked pasta with cherry tomatoes, cucumber, red onion, and chopped basil.
4. **Add Dressing:**
   - Pour the lemon dressing over the pasta salad and toss gently to coat all ingredients evenly.
5. **Finish:**
   - Sprinkle with grated Parmesan cheese and give it a final toss.
6. **Chill and Serve:**
   - Refrigerate the salad for at least 30 minutes to let the flavors meld.
   - Serve chilled or at room temperature.

Enjoy your light and tangy Lemon Basil Pasta Salad!

Mango Avocado Salsa

Ingredients:

- **1 ripe mango**, peeled, pitted, and diced
- **1 ripe avocado**, peeled, pitted, and diced
- **1/4 cup red onion**, finely chopped
- **1/4 cup fresh cilantro**, chopped
- **1 small jalapeño**, seeded and minced (optional, for heat)
- **1 tablespoon lime juice** (about 1 lime)
- **Salt and pepper to taste**

Instructions:

1. **Prepare the Ingredients:**
   - Dice the mango and avocado into small, bite-sized pieces.
   - Finely chop the red onion and cilantro.
   - Mince the jalapeño if you're using it.
2. **Combine the Ingredients:**
   - In a medium bowl, gently mix the diced mango, avocado, red onion, cilantro, and jalapeño.
3. **Add Lime Juice:**
   - Drizzle lime juice over the mixture and gently toss to combine.
4. **Season:**
   - Season with salt and pepper to taste.
5. **Serve:**
   - Serve immediately as a dip with tortilla chips, or use as a topping for grilled chicken, fish, or tacos.

Enjoy your fresh and tangy Mango Avocado Salsa!

Roasted Beet and Goat Cheese Salad

Ingredients:

For the Salad:

- **4 medium beets**, peeled and cut into wedges
- **2 tablespoons olive oil**
- **Salt and pepper to taste**
- **4 cups mixed greens** (such as arugula, spinach, or mesclun)
- **1/2 cup crumbled goat cheese**
- **1/4 cup toasted walnuts** or **pecans** (optional)
- **1/4 cup thinly sliced red onion** (optional)

For the Vinaigrette:

- **3 tablespoons olive oil**
- **1 tablespoon balsamic vinegar**
- **1 tablespoon Dijon mustard**
- **1 teaspoon honey** or **maple syrup**
- **Salt and pepper to taste**

Instructions:

1. **Roast the Beets:**
    - Preheat your oven to 400°F (200°C).
    - Toss the beet wedges with olive oil, salt, and pepper.
    - Arrange the beets on a baking sheet in a single layer.
    - Roast for 35-45 minutes, or until tender and easily pierced with a fork, turning once halfway through. Allow to cool slightly.
2. **Prepare the Vinaigrette:**
    - In a small bowl or jar, whisk together olive oil, balsamic vinegar, Dijon mustard, honey (or maple syrup), salt, and pepper until well combined.
3. **Assemble the Salad:**
    - In a large bowl, toss the mixed greens with some of the vinaigrette.
    - Arrange the roasted beets on top of the greens.
    - Sprinkle with crumbled goat cheese, toasted walnuts or pecans, and red onion (if using).
4. **Serve:**
    - Drizzle the remaining vinaigrette over the salad.
    - Serve immediately.

Enjoy your delicious Roasted Beet and Goat Cheese Salad!

Grilled Vegetable Platter

Ingredients:

- **1 zucchini**, sliced into rounds
- **1 yellow squash**, sliced into rounds
- **1 red bell pepper**, cut into chunks
- **1 green bell pepper**, cut into chunks
- **1 red onion**, cut into wedges
- **8 oz (225g) mushrooms**, whole or halved
- **1 pint cherry tomatoes**
- **2 tablespoons olive oil**
- **1 tablespoon balsamic vinegar**
- **2 cloves garlic**, minced
- **1 teaspoon dried oregano**
- **1 teaspoon dried basil**
- **Salt and pepper to taste**
- **Fresh basil** or **parsley** (for garnish, optional)

Instructions:

1. **Prepare the Vegetables:**
   - Wash and cut the vegetables as needed.
   - Place the zucchini, yellow squash, bell peppers, red onion, mushrooms, and cherry tomatoes in a large bowl.
2. **Make the Marinade:**
   - In a small bowl, whisk together olive oil, balsamic vinegar, minced garlic, dried oregano, dried basil, salt, and pepper.
3. **Marinate the Vegetables:**
   - Pour the marinade over the vegetables and toss to coat evenly.
   - Let the vegetables marinate for at least 15 minutes, or up to 30 minutes for more flavor.
4. **Preheat the Grill:**
   - Preheat your grill to medium-high heat.
5. **Grill the Vegetables:**
   - Arrange the vegetables in a single layer on the grill. You can use a grill basket or skewers for smaller pieces like mushrooms and cherry tomatoes.
   - Grill the vegetables for about 5-7 minutes per side, or until they are tender and have nice grill marks. Turn occasionally to ensure even cooking.
6. **Serve:**
   - Transfer the grilled vegetables to a serving platter.
   - Garnish with fresh basil or parsley if desired.

Enjoy your vibrant and delicious Grilled Vegetable Platter!

Caprese Stuffed Avocados

Ingredients:

- **2 ripe avocados**, halved and pitted
- **1 cup cherry tomatoes**, halved
- **1/4 cup fresh basil leaves**, chopped
- **1/4 cup fresh mozzarella balls** (or diced mozzarella)
- **1 tablespoon balsamic glaze** (store-bought or homemade)
- **1 tablespoon olive oil**
- **Salt and pepper to taste**

Instructions:

1. **Prepare the Ingredients:**
    - Halve and pit the avocados. Carefully scoop out a small portion of the flesh to create more room for stuffing if needed.
    - Halve the cherry tomatoes and chop the fresh basil.
2. **Make the Caprese Filling:**
    - In a bowl, combine the cherry tomatoes, fresh basil, and mozzarella balls (or diced mozzarella).
    - Drizzle with olive oil and season with salt and pepper. Toss gently to combine.
3. **Stuff the Avocados:**
    - Spoon the Caprese mixture into the avocado halves, filling them generously.
4. **Drizzle with Balsamic Glaze:**
    - Drizzle balsamic glaze over the stuffed avocados.
5. **Serve:**
    - Serve immediately for the best texture and flavor. Optionally, garnish with extra basil leaves or a sprinkle of salt and pepper.

Enjoy your fresh and delicious Caprese Stuffed Avocados!

Chilled Cucumber Soup

Ingredients:

- **2 large cucumbers**, peeled, seeded, and chopped
- **1 cup plain Greek yogurt** or **sour cream**
- **1/2 cup fresh dill**, chopped (plus extra for garnish)
- **1/4 cup fresh chives**, chopped
- **2 cloves garlic**, minced
- **1 tablespoon lemon juice** (about 1/2 lemon)
- **1 tablespoon olive oil**
- **Salt and pepper to taste**
- **1 cup cold vegetable or chicken broth**

Instructions:

1. **Prepare the Cucumbers:**
   - Place the chopped cucumbers in a blender or food processor. Blend until smooth.
2. **Mix the Soup:**
   - Add Greek yogurt (or sour cream), fresh dill, chives, minced garlic, lemon juice, olive oil, salt, and pepper to the blender.
   - Blend until all ingredients are well combined and the mixture is smooth.
3. **Adjust Consistency:**
   - If the soup is too thick, add cold vegetable or chicken broth a little at a time until you reach your desired consistency.
4. **Chill:**
   - Transfer the soup to a bowl or pitcher and refrigerate for at least 1 hour, or until well chilled.
5. **Serve:**
   - Garnish with extra fresh dill and serve cold.

Enjoy your light and cooling Chilled Cucumber Soup!

Fruit Salad with Honey Lime Dressing

Ingredients:

For the Fruit Salad:

- **2 cups strawberries**, hulled and halved
- **2 cups blueberries**
- **2 cups pineapple chunks**
- **2 cups kiwi**, peeled and sliced
- **1 cup grapes**, halved
- **1 apple**, diced (optional)
- **1 banana**, sliced (optional)

For the Honey Lime Dressing:

- **1/4 cup honey**
- **2 tablespoons fresh lime juice** (about 1 lime)
- **1 teaspoon lime zest**
- **1/2 teaspoon vanilla extract** (optional)

Instructions:

1. **Prepare the Fruit:**
   - In a large bowl, combine strawberries, blueberries, pineapple chunks, kiwi, grapes, and any optional fruits.
2. **Make the Dressing:**
   - In a small bowl, whisk together honey, lime juice, lime zest, and vanilla extract (if using).
3. **Combine:**
   - Drizzle the honey lime dressing over the fruit salad.
   - Toss gently to coat the fruit evenly with the dressing.
4. **Chill:**
   - Refrigerate the salad for about 30 minutes before serving to let the flavors meld.
5. **Serve:**
   - Serve chilled and enjoy!

Enjoy your sweet and tangy Fruit Salad with Honey Lime Dressing!

Smoked Salmon and Cream Cheese Wraps

Ingredients:

- **4 large flour tortillas** or **wraps**
- **8 oz (225g) cream cheese**, softened
- **4 oz (115g) smoked salmon**, sliced
- **1 tablespoon fresh dill**, chopped (or 1 teaspoon dried dill)
- **1/4 cup red onion**, thinly sliced
- **1 cucumber**, thinly sliced
- **Capers** (optional, for garnish)

Instructions:

1. **Prepare the Spread:**
    - In a bowl, mix the softened cream cheese with fresh dill.
2. **Assemble the Wraps:**
    - Spread a generous layer of the cream cheese mixture over each tortilla.
    - Arrange smoked salmon slices over the cream cheese.
    - Top with red onion slices and cucumber slices.
3. **Roll and Slice:**
    - Roll up each tortilla tightly.
    - Slice the wraps into bite-sized pieces or into halves, depending on your preference.
4. **Garnish (Optional):**
    - Garnish with capers if desired.
5. **Serve:**
    - Serve immediately or refrigerate until ready to serve.

Enjoy your flavorful and easy-to-make Smoked Salmon and Cream Cheese Wraps!

Grilled Peach Salad

Ingredients:

- **4 ripe peaches**, halved and pitted
- **1 tablespoon olive oil**
- **4 cups mixed greens** (such as arugula, spinach, or baby greens)
- **1/4 cup crumbled feta cheese**
- **1/4 cup candied pecans** or **walnuts**
- **1/4 red onion**, thinly sliced
- **1/4 cup fresh basil**, chopped (or mint)

For the Dressing:

- **3 tablespoons balsamic vinegar**
- **2 tablespoons honey**
- **1/4 cup extra virgin olive oil**
- **Salt and pepper to taste**

Instructions:

1. **Grill the Peaches:**
   - Preheat your grill to medium-high heat.
   - Brush the peach halves with olive oil.
   - Grill peaches cut-side down for about 3-4 minutes, or until grill marks appear and the peaches are tender. Remove and let cool slightly.
2. **Prepare the Salad:**
   - In a large bowl, toss the mixed greens with red onion slices and fresh basil.
   - Slice the grilled peaches and add them to the salad.
3. **Make the Dressing:**
   - In a small bowl or jar, whisk together balsamic vinegar, honey, olive oil, salt, and pepper until well combined.
4. **Assemble the Salad:**
   - Drizzle the dressing over the salad.
   - Top with crumbled feta cheese and candied pecans or walnuts.
5. **Serve:**
   - Toss gently to combine and serve immediately.

Enjoy your fresh and flavorful Grilled Peach Salad!

Roasted Garlic Hummus

Ingredients:

- **1 head garlic**
- **1 can (15 oz) chickpeas**, drained and rinsed
- **1/4 cup tahini**
- **1/4 cup fresh lemon juice** (about 1 lemon)
- **1/4 cup extra virgin olive oil**, plus more for roasting
- **1 teaspoon ground cumin**
- **Salt and pepper to taste**
- **1/4 cup water** (adjust for desired consistency)
- **Paprika** and **extra olive oil** for garnish (optional)

Instructions:

1. **Roast the Garlic:**
    - Preheat your oven to 400°F (200°C).
    - Slice the top off the head of garlic to expose the cloves.
    - Drizzle with a little olive oil and wrap in foil.
    - Roast for 30-35 minutes, or until the garlic is soft and caramelized. Let cool, then squeeze the cloves out of their skins.
2. **Prepare the Hummus:**
    - In a food processor, combine the roasted garlic cloves, chickpeas, tahini, lemon juice, olive oil, and ground cumin.
    - Process until smooth, scraping down the sides as needed.
    - Add water a little at a time until you reach your desired consistency.
3. **Season:**
    - Season with salt and pepper to taste.
4. **Serve:**
    - Transfer to a serving bowl.
    - Garnish with a drizzle of olive oil and a sprinkle of paprika if desired.

Enjoy your creamy and flavorful Roasted Garlic Hummus!

Classic Coleslaw

Ingredients:

For the Coleslaw:

- **1 small head green cabbage**, finely shredded (about 6 cups)
- **1 small head red cabbage**, finely shredded (optional, about 2 cups)
- **2 large carrots**, peeled and grated
- **1/2 cup finely chopped red onion** (optional)

For the Dressing:

- **1 cup mayonnaise**
- **2 tablespoons apple cider vinegar**
- **2 tablespoons Dijon mustard**
- **1 tablespoon sugar** (adjust to taste)
- **1/2 teaspoon celery seed** (optional)
- **Salt and pepper to taste**

Instructions:

1. **Prepare the Vegetables:**
   - In a large bowl, combine the shredded green cabbage, red cabbage (if using), grated carrots, and chopped red onion (if using).
2. **Make the Dressing:**
   - In a separate bowl, whisk together mayonnaise, apple cider vinegar, Dijon mustard, sugar, celery seed (if using), salt, and pepper until smooth and well combined.
3. **Combine:**
   - Pour the dressing over the shredded vegetables.
   - Toss well to coat all the vegetables evenly with the dressing.
4. **Chill:**
   - Refrigerate the coleslaw for at least 1 hour before serving to allow the flavors to meld and the slaw to become chilled.
5. **Serve:**
   - Give the coleslaw a quick toss before serving.

Enjoy your classic and crunchy Coleslaw!

Basil Pesto Pasta

Ingredients:

For the Basil Pesto:

- **2 cups fresh basil leaves**, packed
- **1/2 cup pine nuts** (or walnuts as an alternative)
- **1/2 cup grated Parmesan cheese**
- **1/2 cup extra virgin olive oil**
- **3 cloves garlic**
- **Salt and pepper to taste**

For the Pasta:

- **12 oz (340g) pasta** (such as spaghetti, fettuccine, or penne)
- **Salt** (for pasta water)
- **Cherry tomatoes**, halved (optional, for garnish)
- **Additional grated Parmesan cheese** (for serving, optional)

Instructions:

1. **Prepare the Pesto:**
   - In a food processor or blender, combine basil leaves, pine nuts, Parmesan cheese, and garlic.
   - Pulse until the mixture is finely chopped.
   - With the processor running, slowly drizzle in the olive oil until the pesto is smooth and well combined.
   - Season with salt and pepper to taste. Adjust the seasoning as needed.
2. **Cook the Pasta:**
   - Bring a large pot of salted water to a boil.
   - Cook the pasta according to the package instructions until al dente.
   - Reserve about 1/2 cup of pasta cooking water, then drain the pasta.
3. **Combine Pasta and Pesto:**
   - Return the drained pasta to the pot.
   - Add the basil pesto and toss to coat the pasta evenly. If the pesto is too thick, add a bit of the reserved pasta water to reach your desired consistency.
4. **Serve:**
   - Transfer the pasta to serving bowls.
   - Garnish with cherry tomatoes and extra grated Parmesan cheese if desired.

Enjoy your delicious Basil Pesto Pasta!

Buffalo Chicken Lettuce Wraps

Ingredients:

- **1 lb (450g) chicken breast**, cooked and shredded
- **1/2 cup buffalo sauce** (store-bought or homemade)
- **1 tablespoon olive oil**
- **1 small red onion**, finely chopped
- **2 cloves garlic**, minced
- **1/4 cup ranch dressing** or **blue cheese dressing** (optional)
- **1 tablespoon fresh chives** or **parsley**, chopped (optional)
- **1 head iceberg or butter lettuce**, leaves separated

Instructions:

1. **Cook the Chicken:**
    - In a skillet, heat olive oil over medium heat.
    - Add chopped onion and garlic, cooking until softened, about 3-4 minutes.
2. **Add the Chicken:**
    - Stir in the shredded chicken and buffalo sauce.
    - Cook for 2-3 minutes, or until heated through and well-coated with sauce.
3. **Prepare the Lettuce:**
    - Separate the lettuce leaves and wash them thoroughly.
4. **Assemble the Wraps:**
    - Spoon the buffalo chicken mixture onto each lettuce leaf.
    - Drizzle with ranch or blue cheese dressing, if using.
    - Garnish with chopped chives or parsley if desired.
5. **Serve:**
    - Serve immediately as a fun and flavorful appetizer or light meal.

Enjoy your spicy and satisfying Buffalo Chicken Lettuce Wraps!

Marinated Tomato Salad

Ingredients:

- **4-5 ripe tomatoes**, cut into wedges or chunks
- **1/2 red onion**, thinly sliced
- **1/4 cup fresh basil leaves**, chopped
- **1/4 cup extra virgin olive oil**
- **2 tablespoons red wine vinegar** or **balsamic vinegar**
- **1 teaspoon sugar** (optional, to balance acidity)
- **Salt and pepper to taste**
- **1 clove garlic**, minced (optional)

Instructions:

1. **Prepare the Ingredients:**
    - Cut the tomatoes into wedges or chunks, depending on your preference.
    - Thinly slice the red onion.
    - Chop the fresh basil leaves.
2. **Make the Marinade:**
    - In a small bowl, whisk together olive oil, red wine vinegar (or balsamic vinegar), sugar (if using), minced garlic (if using), salt, and pepper until well combined.
3. **Combine and Marinate:**
    - In a large bowl, combine the tomatoes, red onion, and basil.
    - Pour the marinade over the vegetables and toss gently to coat evenly.
4. **Chill:**
    - Let the salad marinate in the refrigerator for at least 30 minutes to allow the flavors to meld.
5. **Serve:**
    - Give the salad a quick toss before serving.

Enjoy your fresh and tangy Marinated Tomato Salad!

Coconut Lime Chicken

Ingredients:

- **4 boneless, skinless chicken breasts** or **thighs**
- **1 can (14 oz) coconut milk**
- **1/4 cup fresh lime juice** (about 2 limes)
- **2 tablespoons soy sauce**
- **2 tablespoons honey** or **maple syrup**
- **2 cloves garlic**, minced
- **1 tablespoon fresh ginger**, minced
- **1 tablespoon olive oil**
- **1 teaspoon ground cumin**
- **1/2 teaspoon ground turmeric** (optional, for color)
- **Salt and pepper to taste**
- **Fresh cilantro**, chopped (for garnish)

Instructions:

1. **Prepare the Marinade:**
    - In a bowl, whisk together coconut milk, lime juice, soy sauce, honey, minced garlic, minced ginger, ground cumin, and turmeric (if using).
2. **Marinate the Chicken:**
    - Place the chicken breasts or thighs in a resealable plastic bag or shallow dish.
    - Pour the marinade over the chicken, ensuring it is well coated.
    - Marinate in the refrigerator for at least 1 hour, or up to 8 hours for more flavor.
3. **Cook the Chicken:**
    - Heat olive oil in a skillet over medium heat.
    - Remove the chicken from the marinade (discard the marinade) and season with salt and pepper.
    - Cook the chicken for 5-7 minutes per side, or until the internal temperature reaches 165°F (74°C) and the chicken is cooked through.
4. **Serve:**
    - Garnish with chopped fresh cilantro before serving.

Enjoy your delicious and aromatic Coconut Lime Chicken!

Sliced Tomato and Burrata Salad

Ingredients:

- **4-5 ripe tomatoes**, sliced (heirloom, beefsteak, or any variety you prefer)
- **8 oz (225g) burrata cheese**
- **2 tablespoons extra virgin olive oil**
- **1 tablespoon balsamic vinegar** or **balsamic glaze**
- **Fresh basil leaves**, for garnish
- **Salt and pepper to taste
- **1/4 teaspoon flaky sea salt** (optional, for finishing)
- **Red pepper flakes** (optional, for a bit of heat)

Instructions:

1. **Prepare the Tomatoes:**
   - Slice the tomatoes into rounds or wedges, depending on your preference.
2. **Arrange the Salad:**
   - On a large serving platter or individual plates, arrange the tomato slices in an overlapping pattern.
3. **Add the Burrata:**
   - Tear or slice the burrata cheese and place it over the tomatoes.
4. **Season:**
   - Drizzle extra virgin olive oil and balsamic vinegar (or balsamic glaze) over the tomatoes and burrata.
   - Season with salt and pepper to taste.
   - Optionally, sprinkle with flaky sea salt and red pepper flakes for added flavor and texture.
5. **Garnish and Serve:**
   - Garnish with fresh basil leaves.

Serve immediately to enjoy the fresh flavors of this Sliced Tomato and Burrata Salad!

Grilled Shrimp and Pineapple Skewers

Ingredients:

- **1 lb (450g) large shrimp**, peeled and deveined
- **1/2 pineapple**, cut into chunks
- **2 tablespoons olive oil**
- **2 tablespoons soy sauce**
- **2 tablespoons honey**
- **2 cloves garlic**, minced
- **1 tablespoon fresh lime juice**
- **1 teaspoon ground cumin**
- **Salt and pepper to taste**
- **Wood or metal skewers**

Instructions:

1. **Prepare the Marinade:**
   - In a bowl, whisk together olive oil, soy sauce, honey, minced garlic, lime juice, ground cumin, salt, and pepper.
2. **Marinate the Shrimp:**
   - Add the shrimp to the marinade and toss to coat evenly.
   - Marinate for 15-30 minutes in the refrigerator.
3. **Prepare the Skewers:**
   - Thread the marinated shrimp and pineapple chunks onto skewers, alternating between shrimp and pineapple.
4. **Preheat the Grill:**
   - Preheat your grill to medium-high heat.
5. **Grill the Skewers:**
   - Place the skewers on the grill and cook for 2-3 minutes per side, or until the shrimp are opaque and cooked through and the pineapple has grill marks.
6. **Serve:**
   - Remove the skewers from the grill and serve immediately.

Enjoy your flavorful and tropical Grilled Shrimp and Pineapple Skewers!

Corn and Black Bean Salad

Ingredients:

- **2 cups corn kernels** (fresh, frozen, or canned; if using frozen, thaw and drain)
- **1 can (15 oz) black beans**, drained and rinsed
- **1 red bell pepper**, diced
- **1/2 red onion**, finely chopped
- **1 avocado**, diced
- **1/4 cup fresh cilantro**, chopped
- **1 tablespoon olive oil**
- **2 tablespoons fresh lime juice** (about 1 lime)
- **1 teaspoon ground cumin**
- **Salt and pepper to taste**

Instructions:

1. **Prepare the Ingredients:**
   - If using fresh corn, cook it briefly in boiling water for 3-4 minutes, then cool and cut the kernels off the cob.
   - Dice the red bell pepper and avocado.
   - Finely chop the red onion and cilantro.
2. **Combine the Salad:**
   - In a large bowl, combine the corn kernels, black beans, red bell pepper, red onion, avocado, and cilantro.
3. **Make the Dressing:**
   - In a small bowl, whisk together olive oil, lime juice, ground cumin, salt, and pepper.
4. **Toss and Serve:**
   - Pour the dressing over the salad and toss gently to combine.
   - Adjust seasoning if necessary.
5. **Serve:**
   - Serve immediately or refrigerate for up to 2 hours to let the flavors meld.

Enjoy your vibrant and tasty Corn and Black Bean Salad!

Chilled Gazpacho

Ingredients:

- **6 ripe tomatoes**, peeled and chopped
- **1 cucumber**, peeled, seeded, and chopped
- **1 red bell pepper**, chopped
- **1 green bell pepper**, chopped
- **1 small red onion**, chopped
- **2 cloves garlic**, minced
- **3 tablespoons olive oil**
- **2 tablespoons red wine vinegar** (or sherry vinegar)
- **1 cup tomato juice** or **vegetable broth**
- **1 teaspoon ground cumin**
- **Salt and pepper to taste**
- **Fresh basil** or **cilantro**, for garnish (optional)

Instructions:

1. **Prepare the Vegetables:**
   - If you prefer a smoother texture, you can peel the tomatoes before chopping them. Otherwise, simply chop them.
   - Peel, seed, and chop the cucumber.
   - Chop the bell peppers and red onion.
   - Mince the garlic.
2. **Blend the Soup:**
   - In a blender or food processor, combine the chopped tomatoes, cucumber, red bell pepper, green bell pepper, red onion, and garlic.
   - Blend until smooth.
3. **Add Seasonings:**
   - Add the olive oil, red wine vinegar, tomato juice (or vegetable broth), and ground cumin to the blender.
   - Blend again until all ingredients are well combined and the soup is smooth.
4. **Season and Chill:**
   - Season with salt and pepper to taste.
   - Transfer the gazpacho to a bowl or pitcher and refrigerate for at least 2 hours, or until well chilled.
5. **Serve:**
   - Garnish with fresh basil or cilantro if desired.
   - Serve cold.

Enjoy your vibrant and refreshing Chilled Gazpacho!

Herbed Lemon Chicken

Ingredients:

- **4 boneless, skinless chicken breasts** or **thighs**
- **2 tablespoons olive oil**
- **1 lemon**, zested and juiced
- **3 cloves garlic**, minced
- **2 tablespoons fresh rosemary**, chopped (or 1 tablespoon dried)
- **2 tablespoons fresh thyme**, chopped (or 1 tablespoon dried)
- **Salt and pepper to taste

Instructions:

1. **Marinate the Chicken:**
   - In a bowl, combine olive oil, lemon zest, lemon juice, minced garlic, rosemary, thyme, salt, and pepper.
   - Place the chicken in the bowl and toss to coat well with the marinade.
   - Cover and refrigerate for at least 30 minutes, or up to 2 hours for more flavor.
2. **Preheat the Oven or Grill:**
   - **Oven Method:** Preheat your oven to 375°F (190°C).
   - **Grill Method:** Preheat your grill to medium-high heat.
3. **Cook the Chicken:**
   - **Oven Method:** Place the marinated chicken on a baking sheet and bake for 20-25 minutes, or until the internal temperature reaches 165°F (74°C) and the chicken is cooked through.
   - **Grill Method:** Grill the chicken for 5-7 minutes per side, or until fully cooked and the internal temperature reaches 165°F (74°C).
4. **Serve:**
   - Let the chicken rest for a few minutes before slicing.
   - Serve with your favorite sides.

Enjoy your delicious and aromatic Herbed Lemon Chicken!

Tomato Mozzarella Skewers

Ingredients:

- 1 pint cherry or grape tomatoes
- 8 oz (225g) **fresh mozzarella balls** (bocconcini or ciliegine)
- **Fresh basil leaves**
- **2 tablespoons extra virgin olive oil**
- **1 tablespoon balsamic glaze** (or balsamic vinegar)
- **Salt and pepper to taste**
- **Wood or metal skewers**

Instructions:

1. **Prepare the Ingredients:**
   - Wash the cherry or grape tomatoes and pat dry.
   - Drain the fresh mozzarella balls if they are packed in liquid.
   - Wash and dry the fresh basil leaves.
2. **Assemble the Skewers:**
   - Thread a cherry tomato onto a skewer, followed by a fresh basil leaf, and then a mozzarella ball.
   - Repeat the process, alternating between tomato, basil, and mozzarella, until the skewer is filled.
   - Repeat with the remaining skewers and ingredients.
3. **Season and Drizzle:**
   - Arrange the skewers on a serving platter.
   - Drizzle with extra virgin olive oil and balsamic glaze.
   - Season with salt and pepper to taste.
4. **Serve:**
   - Serve immediately, or refrigerate until ready to serve.

Enjoy your fresh and flavorful Tomato Mozzarella Skewers!

Peach Iced Tea

Ingredients:

- **4 black tea bags** (or 4 cups loose black tea)
- **4 cups water** (for brewing the tea)
- **2 ripe peaches**, peeled, pitted, and sliced
- **1/2 cup granulated sugar** (adjust to taste)
- **1 cup cold water** (for diluting the tea)
- **Ice**
- **Mint leaves** (for garnish, optional)

Instructions:

1. **Brew the Tea:**
    - In a saucepan, bring 4 cups of water to a boil.
    - Remove from heat and add the tea bags.
    - Let the tea steep for about 5 minutes, then remove the tea bags and discard.
2. **Prepare the Peach Syrup:**
    - In a separate saucepan, combine the sliced peaches and sugar.
    - Cook over medium heat, stirring occasionally, until the peaches are soft and the sugar has dissolved (about 5-7 minutes).
    - Mash the peaches slightly with a spoon or fork to release their juice.
    - Strain the peach mixture through a fine-mesh sieve or cheesecloth into a bowl or pitcher to remove the solids. You should have a peach syrup.
3. **Combine Tea and Peach Syrup:**
    - Add the peach syrup to the brewed tea and stir well.
    - Add 1 cup of cold water to dilute the tea to your desired strength.
4. **Chill and Serve:**
    - Refrigerate the tea until chilled.
    - Serve over ice.
5. **Garnish (Optional):**
    - Garnish with fresh mint leaves or additional peach slices if desired.

Enjoy your refreshing Peach Iced Tea!

Tropical Smoothie Bowl

Ingredients:

- **1 cup frozen mango chunks**
- **1 cup frozen pineapple chunks**
- **1 banana**, sliced
- **1/2 cup coconut milk** (or any milk of your choice)
- **1 tablespoon honey** or **maple syrup** (optional, for sweetness)
- **Toppings**: granola, fresh fruit (like kiwi, berries, or banana), shredded coconut, chia seeds, or nuts

Instructions:

1. **Blend the Smoothie:**
   - In a blender, combine frozen mango, frozen pineapple, banana, and coconut milk.
   - Blend until smooth and creamy. You might need to add a bit more coconut milk if the mixture is too thick.
   - Taste and add honey or maple syrup if desired for extra sweetness.
2. **Assemble the Bowl:**
   - Pour the smoothie into a bowl.
3. **Add Toppings:**
   - Top with granola, fresh fruit, shredded coconut, chia seeds, or nuts according to your preference.
4. **Serve:**
   - Enjoy immediately for the best texture and flavor.

Enjoy your vibrant and nutritious Tropical Smoothie Bowl!

Grilled Teriyaki Chicken

Ingredients:

- **4 boneless, skinless chicken breasts** or **thighs**
- **1/2 cup teriyaki sauce** (store-bought or homemade)
- **2 tablespoons honey**
- **2 tablespoons soy sauce**
- **2 cloves garlic**, minced
- **1 tablespoon fresh ginger**, minced
- **1 tablespoon olive oil** (for grilling)
- **Sesame seeds** and **chopped green onions** for garnish (optional)

Instructions:

1. **Marinate the Chicken:**
   - In a bowl, combine teriyaki sauce, honey, soy sauce, minced garlic, and minced ginger.
   - Place the chicken in a resealable plastic bag or shallow dish and pour the marinade over it.
   - Marinate in the refrigerator for at least 30 minutes, or up to 4 hours for more flavor.
2. **Preheat the Grill:**
   - Preheat your grill to medium-high heat.
   - Brush the grill grates with olive oil to prevent sticking.
3. **Grill the Chicken:**
   - Remove the chicken from the marinade (discard the marinade).
   - Grill the chicken for 5-7 minutes per side, or until the internal temperature reaches 165°F (74°C) and the chicken is cooked through.
4. **Serve:**
   - Remove the chicken from the grill and let it rest for a few minutes.
   - Garnish with sesame seeds and chopped green onions if desired.

Enjoy your delicious and savory Grilled Teriyaki Chicken!

Sweet Corn Salad

Ingredients:

- **4 cups fresh corn kernels** (about 4 ears of corn; or use frozen, thawed)
- **1 red bell pepper**, diced
- **1/2 red onion**, finely chopped
- **1 avocado**, diced
- **1/4 cup fresh cilantro**, chopped
- **2 tablespoons lime juice** (about 1 lime)
- **2 tablespoons olive oil**
- **Salt and pepper to taste**

Instructions:

1. **Cook the Corn:**
    - If using fresh corn, cook it in boiling water for 3-4 minutes until tender. Cool and cut the kernels off the cob. If using frozen corn, thaw and drain it.
2. **Combine the Ingredients:**
    - In a large bowl, mix the corn kernels, diced red bell pepper, chopped red onion, diced avocado, and chopped cilantro.
3. **Dress the Salad:**
    - In a small bowl, whisk together lime juice, olive oil, salt, and pepper.
    - Pour the dressing over the salad and toss gently to combine.
4. **Serve:**
    - Serve immediately or refrigerate for up to 2 hours to let the flavors meld.

Enjoy your fresh and sweet Corn Salad!

Chicken Caesar Wraps

Ingredients:

- **2 cups cooked chicken breast**, diced or shredded (grilled or rotisserie chicken works well)
- **1 cup Caesar dressing**
- **1/2 cup grated Parmesan cheese**
- **2 cups romaine lettuce**, chopped
- **1/4 cup croutons**, crushed (optional, for crunch)
- **4 large flour tortillas** or **wraps**

Instructions:

1. **Prepare the Chicken Mixture:**
   - In a large bowl, toss the cooked chicken with Caesar dressing until well coated.
   - Stir in grated Parmesan cheese.
2. **Assemble the Wraps:**
   - Lay out the tortillas on a flat surface.
   - Evenly distribute the chopped romaine lettuce over each tortilla.
   - Spoon the chicken mixture on top of the lettuce.
   - Sprinkle with crushed croutons if using.
3. **Wrap and Serve:**
   - Fold in the sides of the tortilla and roll it up tightly from one end to the other.
   - Slice in half if desired.

Enjoy your easy and tasty Chicken Caesar Wraps!

Strawberry Shortcake

Ingredients:

For the Biscuits:

- **2 cups all-purpose flour**
- **1/4 cup granulated sugar**
- **1 tablespoon baking powder**
- **1/2 teaspoon salt**
- **1/2 cup cold unsalted butter**, cut into small pieces
- **2/3 cup milk** (plus a little extra for brushing)
- **1 teaspoon vanilla extract**

For the Strawberries:

- **4 cups fresh strawberries**, hulled and sliced
- **1/4 cup granulated sugar**

For the Whipped Cream:

- **1 cup heavy cream**
- **2 tablespoons powdered sugar**
- **1 teaspoon vanilla extract**

Instructions:

1. **Prepare the Strawberries:**
    - Toss the sliced strawberries with 1/4 cup sugar.
    - Let them sit for at least 30 minutes to allow the juices to release.
2. **Make the Biscuits:**
    - Preheat your oven to 425°F (220°C).
    - In a large bowl, whisk together flour, sugar, baking powder, and salt.
    - Cut in the butter using a pastry cutter or your fingers until the mixture resembles coarse crumbs.
    - Stir in milk and vanilla extract until just combined.
    - Turn the dough out onto a floured surface, knead lightly, and roll out to about 1-inch thickness.
    - Cut into rounds and place on a baking sheet.
    - Brush the tops with a little milk.
    - Bake for 12-15 minutes or until golden brown. Allow to cool.
3. **Whip the Cream:**
    - In a chilled bowl, beat the heavy cream, powdered sugar, and vanilla extract until soft peaks form.
4. **Assemble the Shortcake:**
    - Split the biscuits in half.
    - Spoon some strawberries and their juice over the bottom half of each biscuit.

- Top with a dollop of whipped cream.
- Place the top half of the biscuit on top.

Enjoy your classic Strawberry Shortcake!

Avocado and Tomato Quesadillas

Ingredients:

- **4 flour tortillas**
- **1 cup shredded cheese** (such as cheddar, Monterey Jack, or a blend)
- **1 ripe avocado**, sliced
- **1 large tomato**, sliced
- **1 tablespoon olive oil** or **butter**
- **Salt and pepper to taste**
- **Optional: Fresh cilantro**, chopped (for garnish)
- **Optional: Sour cream** and **salsa** (for serving)

Instructions:

1. **Prepare the Filling:**
   - Slice the avocado and tomato. Season the tomato slices with a pinch of salt and pepper.
2. **Assemble the Quesadillas:**
   - Heat a large skillet over medium heat and add a small amount of olive oil or butter.
   - Place one tortilla in the skillet.
   - Sprinkle half of the shredded cheese evenly over the tortilla.
   - Arrange avocado and tomato slices on top of the cheese.
   - Sprinkle with the remaining cheese and top with another tortilla.
3. **Cook the Quesadillas:**
   - Cook for 2-3 minutes, or until the bottom tortilla is golden brown and the cheese is starting to melt.
   - Carefully flip the quesadilla and cook for another 2-3 minutes on the other side, until golden brown and the cheese is fully melted.
4. **Serve:**
   - Remove from the skillet and let cool slightly before slicing into wedges.
   - Garnish with chopped cilantro if desired and serve with sour cream and salsa.

Enjoy your flavorful and satisfying Avocado and Tomato Quesadillas!

Grilled Lobster Tails

Ingredients:

- **4 lobster tails**
- **1/4 cup melted butter**
- **2 cloves garlic**, minced
- **1 tablespoon lemon juice** (about 1/2 lemon)
- **1 teaspoon smoked paprika** (optional)
- **1 teaspoon dried parsley** or **fresh parsley**, chopped
- **Salt and pepper to taste**
- **Lemon wedges**, for serving

Instructions:

1. **Prepare the Lobster Tails:**
   - Using kitchen scissors, cut the top shell of each lobster tail lengthwise, from the base to the tip. Be careful not to cut all the way through.
   - Gently pull the shell apart to expose the lobster meat. You can also gently lift the meat from the shell and place it on top for even grilling.
2. **Make the Butter Mixture:**
   - In a small bowl, mix together melted butter, minced garlic, lemon juice, smoked paprika (if using), dried parsley, salt, and pepper.
3. **Preheat the Grill:**
   - Preheat your grill to medium-high heat.
4. **Grill the Lobster Tails:**
   - Brush the lobster meat with some of the butter mixture.
   - Place the lobster tails on the grill, shell-side down. Close the lid and cook for 5-7 minutes.
   - Open the lid and brush the lobster meat with more butter mixture.
   - Flip the lobster tails and cook for another 3-5 minutes, or until the lobster meat is opaque and firm (the internal temperature should reach 145°F or 63°C).
5. **Serve:**
   - Remove from the grill and brush with any remaining butter mixture.
   - Serve with lemon wedges for extra flavor.

Enjoy your perfectly grilled lobster tails!

Mango Coconut Chia Pudding

Ingredients:

- **1/2 cup chia seeds**
- **1 cup coconut milk** (canned or carton)
- **1/2 cup mango puree** (fresh or frozen)
- **2 tablespoons maple syrup** or **honey** (adjust to taste)
- **1/2 teaspoon vanilla extract** (optional)
- **Fresh mango chunks** and **toasted coconut flakes** for topping

Instructions:

1. **Prepare the Chia Mixture:**
    - In a bowl, whisk together chia seeds, coconut milk, mango puree, maple syrup (or honey), and vanilla extract if using.
    - Stir well to ensure there are no clumps of chia seeds.
2. **Refrigerate:**
    - Cover the bowl and refrigerate for at least 4 hours, or overnight. The chia seeds will absorb the liquid and expand, creating a pudding-like texture.
3. **Serve:**
    - Stir the pudding before serving. If it's too thick, you can add a bit more coconut milk to reach your desired consistency.
    - Top with fresh mango chunks and toasted coconut flakes.

Enjoy your refreshing and tropical Mango Coconut Chia Pudding!

Ginger Peach Salsa

Ingredients:

- **3 ripe peaches**, peeled, pitted, and diced
- **1 small red onion**, finely chopped
- **1 red bell pepper**, diced
- **1 jalapeño pepper**, seeded and minced (adjust for heat preference)
- **1 tablespoon fresh ginger**, minced
- **2 tablespoons fresh lime juice** (about 1 lime)
- **1 tablespoon honey** or **maple syrup** (optional, for extra sweetness)
- **1/4 cup fresh cilantro**, chopped
- **Salt and pepper to taste**

Instructions:

1. **Prepare the Ingredients:**
    - Peel, pit, and dice the peaches.
    - Finely chop the red onion and dice the red bell pepper.
    - Seed and mince the jalapeño pepper.
    - Mince the fresh ginger.
2. **Combine the Ingredients:**
    - In a large bowl, mix together the diced peaches, chopped red onion, diced red bell pepper, minced jalapeño, and minced ginger.
3. **Add the Dressing:**
    - Stir in fresh lime juice and honey (if using).
    - Mix well to combine.
4. **Season and Garnish:**
    - Add fresh cilantro and season with salt and pepper to taste.
    - Mix again.
5. **Chill and Serve:**
    - Let the salsa sit for at least 30 minutes in the refrigerator to allow the flavors to meld.
    - Serve chilled or at room temperature.

Enjoy your Ginger Peach Salsa with grilled dishes, seafood, or simply with tortilla chips!

Lemon Blueberry Muffins

Ingredients:

For the Muffins:

- 1 1/2 cups all-purpose flour
- 1/2 cup granulated sugar
- 2 teaspoons baking powder
- 1/2 teaspoon baking soda
- 1/4 teaspoon salt
- 1/2 cup unsalted butter, melted and cooled
- 1/2 cup plain Greek yogurt or sour cream
- 2 large eggs
- 1 tablespoon lemon zest (about 1 lemon)
- 1 tablespoon lemon juice (about 1 lemon)
- 1 cup fresh or frozen blueberries

For the Lemon Glaze (optional):

- 1/2 cup powdered sugar
- 2 tablespoons lemon juice

Instructions:

1. **Preheat the Oven:**
   - Preheat your oven to 375°F (190°C).
   - Line a muffin tin with paper liners or lightly grease it.
2. **Mix Dry Ingredients:**
   - In a medium bowl, whisk together flour, sugar, baking powder, baking soda, and salt.
3. **Mix Wet Ingredients:**
   - In a large bowl, whisk together melted butter, Greek yogurt (or sour cream), eggs, lemon zest, and lemon juice.
4. **Combine Ingredients:**
   - Add the dry ingredients to the wet ingredients and stir until just combined. Be careful not to overmix.
   - Gently fold in the blueberries.
5. **Fill Muffin Tin:**
   - Divide the batter evenly among the muffin cups, filling each about 2/3 full.
6. **Bake:**
   - Bake for 18-22 minutes, or until a toothpick inserted into the center of a muffin comes out clean.
7. **Cool:**
   - Let the muffins cool in the pan for 5 minutes, then transfer to a wire rack to cool completely.
8. **Optional Glaze:**

- In a small bowl, mix powdered sugar with lemon juice until smooth.
- Drizzle the glaze over the cooled muffins.

Enjoy your delicious Lemon Blueberry Muffins with a cup of tea or coffee!

www.ingramcontent.com/pod-product-compliance
Lightning Source LLC
LaVergne TN
LVHW081320060526
838201LV00055B/2393